CAMBRIDGE UNIVERSITY PRESS

CAMBRIDGE PRIMARY
Global Perspectives

Learner's Skills Book 1

Adrian Ravenscroft & Achama Mathew

Shaftesbury Road, Cambridge CB2 8BS, United Kingdom

One Liberty Plaza, 20th Floor, New York, NY 10006, USA

477 Williamstown Road, Port Melbourne, VIC 3207, Australia

314–321, 3rd Floor, Plot 3, Splendor Forum, Jasola District Centre, New Delhi – 110025, India

103 Penang Road, #05–06/07, Visioncrest Commercial, Singapore 238467

Cambridge University Press is part of the University of Cambridge.

It furthers the University's mission by disseminating knowledge in the pursuit of education, learning and research at the highest international levels of excellence.

www.cambridge.org
Information on this title: www.cambridge.org/9781009354158

© Cambridge University Press & Assessment 2024

This publication is in copyright. Subject to statutory exception and to the provisions of relevant collective licensing agreements, no reproduction of any part may take place without the written permission of Cambridge University Press.

First published 2024

20 19 18 17 16 15 14 13 12 11 10 9 8 7 6 5 4 3

Printed in Poland by Opolgraf

A catalogue record for this publication is available from the British Library

ISBN 978-1-009-35415-8 Learner's Skills Book 1 Paperback with Digital Access (1 Year)
ISBN 978-1-009-35803-3 Learner Skills Book 1 – eBook

Cambridge University Press has no responsibility for the persistence or accuracy of URLs for external or third-party internet websites referred to in this publication, and does not guarantee that any content on such websites is, or will remain, accurate or appropriate. Information regarding prices, travel timetables, and other factual information given in this work is correct at the time of first printing but Cambridge University Press does not guarantee the accuracy of such information thereafter.

Cambridge International copyright material in this publication is reproduced under licence and remains the intellectual property of Cambridge Assessment International Education.

....

NOTICE TO TEACHERS
It is illegal to reproduce any part of this work in material form (including photocopying and electronic storage) except under the following circumstances:
(i) where you are abiding by a licence granted to your school or institution by the Copyright Licensing Agency;
(ii) where no such licence exists, or where you wish to exceed the terms of a licence, and you have gained the written permission of Cambridge University Press;
(iii) where you are allowed to reproduce without permission under the provisions of Chapter 3 of the Copyright, Designs and Patents Act 1988, which covers, for example, the reproduction of short passages within certain types of educational anthology and reproduction for the purposes of setting examination questions.

2023 CAMBRIDGE DEDICATED TEACHER AWARDS

Teachers play an important part in shaping futures.
Our Dedicated Teacher Awards recognise the hard work that teachers put in every day.

Thank you to everyone who nominated this year; we have been inspired and moved by all of your stories. Well done to all of our nominees for your dedication to learning and for inspiring the next generation of thinkers, leaders and innovators.

CONGRATULATIONS TO OUR INCREDIBLE WINNERS!

WINNER — Central & Southern Africa
Akeem Badru
St Michael R.C.M Primary School, Ogunpa Lunloye, Nigeria

Regional Winner: East & South Asia
Gaurav Sharma
FirstSteps School, India

Regional Winner: North & South America
Nathalie Roy
Glasgow Middle School, United States

Regional Winner: Australia, New Zealand & South-East Asia
Goh Kok Ming
SJKC Hua Lian 1, Malaysia

Regional Winner: Middle East & North Africa
Uzma Siraj
Future World School, Pakistan

Regional Winner: Europe
Selçuk Yusuf Arslan
Atatürk MTAL, Turkey

For more information about our dedicated teachers and their stories, go to **dedicatedteacher.cambridge.org**

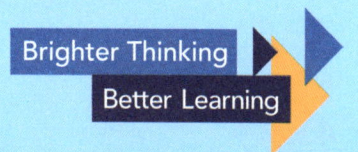

Endorsement statement

Endorsement indicates that a resource has passed Cambridge International's rigorous quality-assurance process and is suitable to support the delivery of a Cambridge International curriculum framework. However, endorsed resources are not the only suitable materials available to support teaching and learning, and are not essential to be used to achieve the qualification. Resource lists found on the Cambridge International website will include this resource and other endorsed resources.

Any example answers to questions taken from past question papers, practice questions, accompanying marks and mark schemes included in this resource have been written by the authors and are for guidance only. They do not replicate examination papers. In examinations the way marks are awarded may be different. Any references to assessment and/or assessment preparation are the publisher's interpretation of the curriculum framework requirements. Examiners will not use endorsed resources as a source of material for any assessment set by Cambridge International.

While the publishers have made every attempt to ensure that advice on the qualification and its assessment is accurate, the official curriculum framework, specimen assessment materials and any associated assessment guidance materials produced by the awarding body are the only authoritative source of information and should always be referred to for definitive guidance. Cambridge International recommends that teachers consider using a range of teaching and learning resources based on their own professional judgement of their learners' needs.

Cambridge International has not paid for the production of this resource, nor does Cambridge International receive any royalties from its sale. For more information about the endorsement process, please visit www.cambridgeinternational.org/endorsed-resources

Contents

Introduction	6
How to use this book	8
1 What can families teach us?	10
2 What kind of garden would be best?	34
3 What do we know about jobs?	54
4 How can we save water?	80
Glossary	108

Introduction

Introduction

Welcome to Stage 1 of **Cambridge Primary Global Perspectives**. We hope you will find the projects in this book interesting.

You are going to work on four projects. The projects in this book help you understand new things.

The projects are about:

- your family
- gardens
- jobs people do
- saving water.

There are four children in the book.

They try out all of the projects.

Here is Zara. Here is Marcus. Here is Arun. Here is Sofia.

You do not need to learn facts.
You will need to help people.

You will learn how to:
- find out new facts
- find out what people think
- talk to lots of people
- think about what you do.

You will need to work in different ways:
- sometimes you will work on your own
- sometimes you will work with a partner or a group
- sometimes you will learn in the classroom
- sometimes you will learn in different places.

There are lots of ways to do well:
- think about your own ideas
- think about other people's ideas
- help other learners to learn
- try out new ways to learn
- help other people to learn new things.

We hope you will enjoy the projects in this book!

Adrian Ravenscroft and Achama Mathew

How to use this book

How to use this book

In this book you will find lots of different things to help your learning.

You will see a picture and discussion at the start of each project. →

Getting started
With your class, look at the pictures and talk about the questions. • Who are the people in the pictures? • What are they doing? • What things do you like doing with your family?

The learning goals show you what you will learn. There is space for you to show what you think at the end of the lesson. There is also space for your teacher to say what you have learned. →

Learning goals		
Our learning goals	I think ☺ ☹	My teacher thinks ☺ ☹
I can ask questions to find out about people's lives		

This tells you what the key words are. Key words are in the glossary. The glossary is at the back of the book. You can find out what the key words mean there. →   chart   popular

How to use this book

Here are things to do.
They will help you learn.

> **What questions will we ask?**
>
> 1. Look at Sofia, Arun and Zara's garden again.
>   Marcus wants to find out more about their garden.
>   He thinks of three questions.
>   Draw 🙂 next to the good questions.
>   Draw ☹ next to a question that is not useful.
>
> *How did you make the tree?*
> *How old are you?*
> *Do butterflies like these flowers?*

Interesting facts and information.

> **Did you know?**
>
> Did you know that plants need food? **Compost** is a very good food for plants. You can make it in a compost box in your garden. It's easy! Just put your banana skins, apple cores and vegetable peel in the box. Mix it up with a spade. After a few months, you will have lovely compost!

Useful words.
You can use these words.

> a very good source   not a good source
> quite a good source   because

 Audio is available on Cambridge GO and in the Teacher's Resource.

 Video is available on Cambridge GO and in the Teacher's Resource.

 Your teacher will have access to free supporting resources through Cambridge GO – the home for all your Cambridge digital content. Visit cambridge.org/go

9

1 ▶ What can families teach us?

Getting started

With your class, look at the pictures and talk about the questions.

- Who are the people in the pictures?
- What are they doing?
- What things do you like doing with your family?

1   What can families teach us?

11

1 What can families teach us?

1.1 Who is in my family?

Learning goals

Our learning goals	I think	My teacher thinks
I can say who is in my family	☺ 😐	☺ 😐 ....
I can find out if we all use the same names for family members	☺ 😐	☺ 😐 ....

1 What can families teach us?

Who are my family members?

1 Look at the picture of Arun's family again. Five people live in Arun's home: Arun, his sister, his uncle, his father and his mother.

family member

Draw the people who live with you in your home. Or you can stick in a photograph.

Write who those people are by writing their names beneath your drawing or photo.

2 Write the names of some **family members** who do not live with you. Do you know where they live? Tell your partner.

....

....

....

1 What can families teach us?

What do I call my adult family members?

1 Read what Marcus and Arun say.

What do you call your older family members? Write it in the table.

Family member	What I call them
Grandmother	
Father	

1   What can families teach us?

2   Are there other adults who are not family members who look after you too? Write what you call them here.

....

Do we all have the same names for our family members?

Work in a group. Say what you wrote in your chart. Do all the children in your group use the **same** names for family members?

Write the name of one family member where you all have the **same** name.

....

Write the name of one family member where you all have **different** names.

....

Did you know?

There are lots of **different** names for a grandmother. In Italy, they call her Nonna. In South Africa, they call her Ouma or Gogo. In Indonesia, she is Nenek.

same

different

1 What can families teach us?

1.2 What have my family members taught me to do?

Learning goals		
Our learning goals	**I think**	**My teacher thinks**
I can talk about what I have learned from family members	☺ 😐	☺ 😐
I can record answers in a chart	☺ 😐	☺ 😐

What can we learn from our family members?

You are going to watch a video.
You will see children doing things with their families.

16

1   What can families teach us?

1   Look at the pictures from the video. Talk about them.
    - What are the children learning to do?
    - Who is showing them how to do it?
    - Can you do the things you see in the pictures? Who showed you how?

2   Think of two more things that you have learned how to do.
    Who showed you how?

How can I fill in a chart?

1   Zara has learned lots of things from the people who look after her. She has written them in a chart. Look at Zara's chart.

taught

	Can I do it? ✓	Who taught me how?
brush my teeth	✓	Mum and Papa
fly a kite	✓	Papa
water the plants	✓	Mrs Ghulam

What things has Zara learned to do? Who taught her?

17

1   What can families teach us?

2   Fill in the chart for yourself.

Put a tick (✓) in the box of the things that you have learned to do. Write the name of the person who taught you.

	Can I do it? ✓	Who taught me how?
brush my teeth		
fly a kite		
water the plants		

Finish the chart. Draw or write two more things that you can do. Write who taught you to do the things.

1   What can families teach us?

3   Talk to a partner about your chart.

Share with your partner what you have learned from different family members.

Put a tick (✓) in the box for same or different. Has your partner learned the same things as you or different things?

> I have learned how to fly a kite. My grandad taught me.

same ☐

different ☐

4   Have you got a younger brother, sister, cousin or friend?

What could you teach them to do? Write your ideas here.

....

....

How can I show I am grateful?

grateful

1   Our family members share a lot of things with us.
We learn a lot of things from them.

Marcus has thought of some ways to show his family that he is grateful. What do you think about Marcus's ideas? Draw 🙂 if it is a good idea. Draw ☹ if it is not a good idea.

Buy them a new car. ☐   Say 'Thank you'. ☐

Do something helpful at home. ☐

19

1 What can families teach us?

2 How could you show your family that you are grateful?
   Draw or write your idea here.

> 1.3 What can I find out in an interview?

Learning goals

Our learning goals	I think	My teacher thinks
		☺ ☹
I can ask questions to find out about people's lives	☺ ☹	....

What questions can we ask in an interview?

1 You are going to **interview** a visitor to your class. You will ask them questions to find out about their life when they were a child.

First, listen to this interview. Sofia is talking to her grandfather. What questions does she ask?

1 What can families teach us?

2 Listen again. Answer these questions with your partner.

a What things did Sofia's grandfather do when he was a child?

b Which people taught Sofia's grandfather how to do different things?

c How was Sofia's grandfather's life different from your life?

How do we interview a visitor?

1 You are going to do your own interview. You will interview a visitor.

Our visitor's name is ....

2 Work in a small group.

Think of what you would like to know about your visitor's life as a child. Make up some questions.

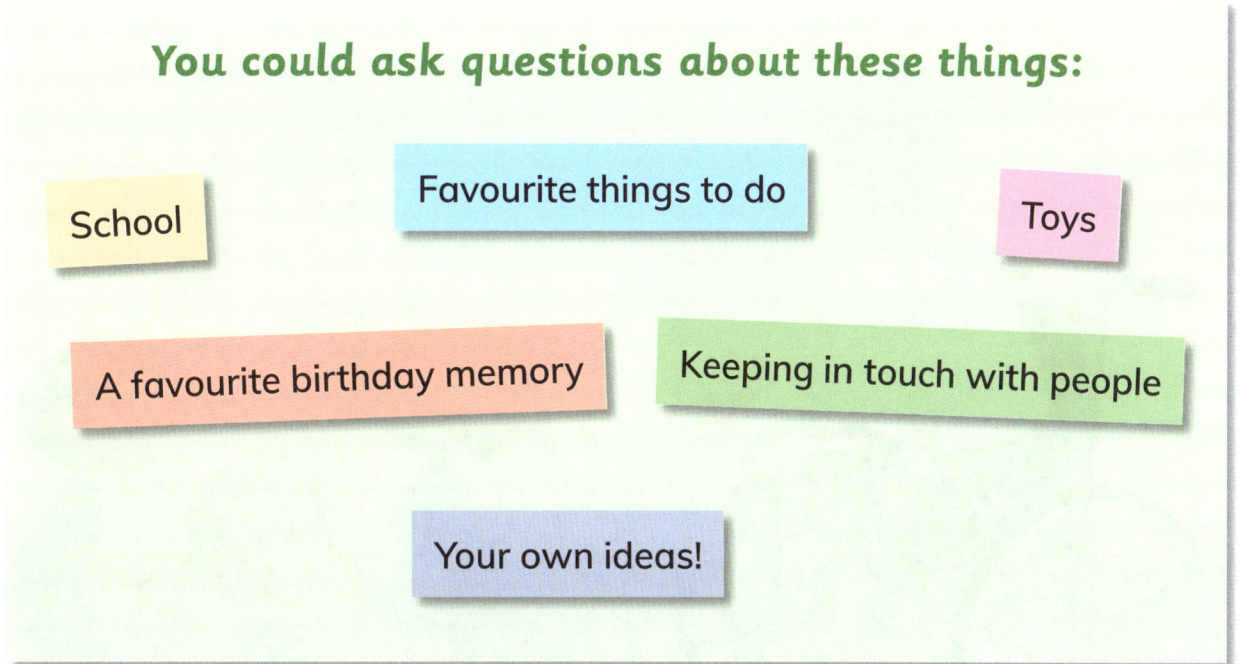

21

1   What can families teach us?

3   Decide which your best questions are. Make a list.

    1   ....
        .... Name: ....

    2   ....
        .... Name: ....

    3   ....
        .... Name: ....

    4   ....
        .... Name: ....

4   Decide who will ask each question. Write their name next to the question.

5   With your teacher, practise asking the questions.

1   What can families teach us?

6   Carry out the interview. Ask the visitor your questions.

> That's interesting!   Can you tell me more about ….?
>
> Thank you for talking to us.

What did we learn from the interview?

1   Put a tick (✓) in the box for the information you found out.

- [ ] their family
- [ ] their school
- [ ] jobs their parents did
- [ ] games they played
- [ ] the toys they had
- [ ] their friends
- [ ] their house
- [ ] how they helped at home

Did you find out some other information? Write or draw it here.

2   Answer the questions. Circle Yes or No.

Did you like doing the interview?   Yes / No

Did you find out some interesting information?   Yes / No

Share the reasons for your answers with the class.

1 What can families teach us?

3   Now you can interview someone in your family or someone who looks after you. Who would you like to interview? Write their name here.

....

> 1.4 What else can I find out from my family members?

Learning goals		
Our learning goals	I think	My teacher thinks
I can learn stories, games and interesting facts from older people	☺ ☺	☺ ☺ ....

What can we find out about a festival?

Arun, Zara and Sofia wanted to learn some more things from the people who look after them. Arun's grandmother showed him a photo. She told him about a *festival* called Diwali.

1   Arun calls his grandmother Naani. She grew up in Delhi in India. Look at the photo that Naani showed Arun.

Listen to Arun telling us what his Naani said about the photo. Answer these questions.

   a   What festival is she talking about?

   b   What did Naani's family do during this festival?

24

1 What can families teach us?

2   Listen again. Answer these questions with your partner.
   a   What is the most interesting thing you have learned about Diwali?
   b   Why do you think Naani said it was the best time of the year?

What stories can we find out?

Zara's aunt told her a story about her father and a bell.

Zara wanted to share the story with her friends at school.
Her teacher helped her to write it down.

1   Listen to your teacher read Zara's aunt's story.

My aunt lived in a village far from the city. Her father was a doctor. All the people in the village called him Doctor Uncle. There was a big bell on the door of my aunt's house. People would ring the bell to let Doctor Uncle know that they were waiting to see him.

One day an old man came to see Doctor Uncle. His legs were hurting and he could not walk. Doctor Uncle checked the old man's legs. He took out a big thorn, put a bandage on and gave the old man a walking stick. The old man felt better. On his way out, he rang the bell loudly. My aunt went out to see what had happened. The old man said he was so happy that he was feeling better, he rang the bell to say 'thank you' to Doctor Uncle. He wanted everyone in the village to know that the doctor had helped him. From that day on, my aunt heard the bell ring every day, many times. All the people of the village would ring the bell on their way out …just to say thank you to Doctor Uncle!

1 What can families teach us?

2 Read the questions about the story. Then answer the questions.

   a Who told this story to Zara? ....

   b How did the doctor help the old man? Tick (✓) the box.

      • He gave him some medicine. ☐

      • He took out a thorn. ☐

   c Why did people ring the bell? ....

   ....

   ....

   d Do you think he was a good doctor? Tick (✓) the box.

      Yes ☐   No ☐

      Why do you think that? ....

      ....

      ....

3 Talk to your partner. Who tells you stories in your family?
   What are the stories about? What is interesting about the stories?

What games can we find out about?

Sofia's neighbour Maria told Sofia about a game. It is a game Maria played with her family many years ago. The game is called 'Dots and Boxes'. Sofia wanted to tell her friends about the game. Her teacher helped her write down the instructions.

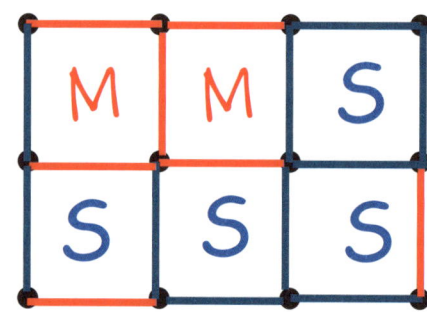

1 What can families teach us?

This is the game that Sofia played with Maria.

1   Read the instructions.

> ## HOW TO PLAY
> ## DOTS AND BOXES
>
> You can play this game with two, three or four players.
>
> You have a sheet of paper with dots like this:
>
>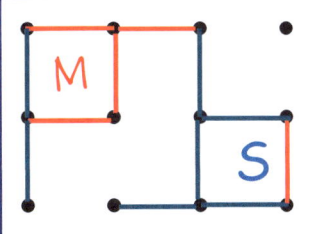
>
> Each person needs a pencil.
>
> Players take turns to draw a line between two dots. Each player can draw only one line when it is their turn.
>
> The aim is to join the lines to make squares.
>
> If you make a square, you can write the first letter of your name in the square. You win that square.
>
> The person who wins the most squares is the **winner!**

Look at the game that Sofia played with her neighbour Maria.
Who won that game?

Play the game with your partner!

1 What can families teach us?

2 Talk to your partner. Answer the questions.

   a   Do you like this game? Who could you play it with?

   b   Do you play games with your family or your friends? What games do you play? Who taught you to play the games?

   c   Are the games you play similar to Dots and Boxes?

   d   How are they different?

> 1.5 How can we show what we have learned?

Learning goals

Our learning goals	I think	My teacher thinks
I can show other people what I have learned from my family	☺ 😐	☺ 😐

How can we make a display about the people who taught us things?

You are going to make a **display** with your class. The display will show the things that you have learned from someone in your family or another older person.

display

1   What can families teach us?

Look at what Marcus made for his class display. He drew a picture of his grandmother. Then he wrote about what she taught him.

> This is my grandmother.
> I call her Nanna.
>
> She told me a story. She looked after a little bird. It fell out of its nest.

1   Choose an older person who has taught you something in this project. Write their name here.

    ....

    What has the older person taught you?

    A story ☐   Information about their childhood ☐

    A game ☐   Information about a festival ☐

    Something else: ....

2   Draw a picture of the older person. Write their name. Write what they have taught you.

1 What can families teach us?

How will we tell people more about what we learned?

1 How could Marcus give his class more information about what he learned from his grandmother?

Write your idea here:

....

....

2 How can **you** tell people about what you have learned? Discuss your ideas with a partner. (Circle) the ideas that you like.

> Talk about it   Write about it
>
> Act it out   Draw a picture
>
> My idea ....

Write what you have decided.

I will ....

....

How can we answer questions from our classmates?

1 Your classmates will share what they learned from an older person. Think of good questions to ask.

1 What can families teach us?

2 What questions did you ask?

....

....

Did your classmate give you a good answer? Draw a star or a face.

- a very good answer ☆
- quite a good answer ☺

3 Now it is your turn to share what you learned! Your classmates will ask you a question. Listen carefully. Answer their question.

What question did they ask?

....

Did you give a good answer?
Draw a star or a face.

> 1.6 What did we enjoy doing?

Learning goals		
Our learning goals	**I think**	**My teacher thinks**
I can talk about something I liked	☺ ☹	☺ ☹ ....

1 What can families teach us?

What have I found out about families?

In each box, write or draw something you found out.

New things I have found out	
Where my family members live	Things about their childhood
Different names for family members	Stories, festivals, games

1 What can families teach us?

How did I feel about it?

Read about the things you did in this project. Draw a star or a face.

I loved it ☆   I liked it 😊   I didn't like it much

I talked about the names we use for family members.		I did an interview.	
I said what my family helped me learn.		I found out information from older family members.	
I filled in a table.		I made a display.	
I talked about our display.		I learned to play a new game.	

Have I learned how to do something new?

Marcus learned how to do something new in his project.

I have learned how to make a display

Write one thing you learned how to do.

I have learned how ....

2 What kind of garden would be best?

Getting started

1. Read and listen to the chant.

   Repeat the chant out loud. Point to the people doing the things in the chant.

2. Look at the picture. Point and say the things you can see.

   What things can people do in a garden?

2 What kind of garden would be best?

2.1 What is a garden?

Learning goals

Our learning goals	I think	My teacher thinks
I can say what I know about gardens	☺ 😐	☺ 😐 ....

What can we do in a garden?

Look at the pictures of gardens.

1   Ask and answer these questions with a partner.

   a   What can you see in these gardens?
   b   What are the people doing?
   c   How are the gardens different?
   d   How are the gardens **similar**?

similar

36

2 What kind of garden would be best?

What different kinds of garden are there?

 1 Listen to the people talking about their gardens.
Draw a line from the person to their garden.

 Shazia

 Afua

 Romario

2 Finish the sentences. Use these words to help you.

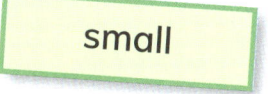

small   butterfly   vegetable

a   Shazia has a .... garden.

b   Afua has a .... garden.

c   Romario likes visiting a .... garden.

37

> 2 What kind of garden would be best?

3 Which garden in the photos is best for Marcus?
   Write 1, 2 or 3.

   Garden .... is best for Marcus.

4 Which garden is best for you? Tell your partner.

What kind of garden have you seen?

1 Draw a garden that you have seen.
   If you want to, draw somebody in the garden doing something.

2 Talk to your partner about the garden you have drawn.

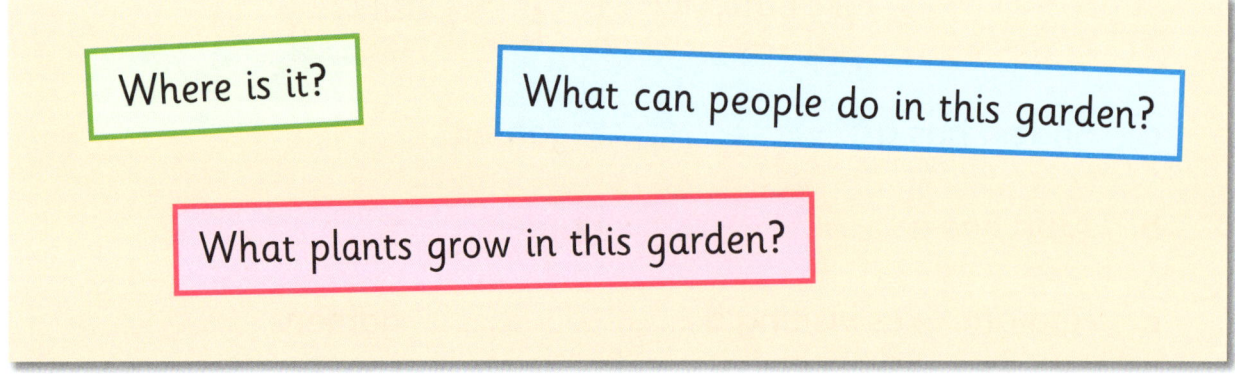

2.2 How can I find out what children in my class think about gardens?

Learning goals

Our learning goals	I think	My teacher thinks
I can make a chart that shows children's ideas	☺ 😐	☺ 😐

How can we use pictures to show our ideas?

1   Sofia and her friends have lots of ideas for things to put in their school garden. They have drawn a little picture for each idea:

minibeast hotel

popular

chart

The children want to find out which is the most popular idea. They make a chart like this:

2 What kind of garden would be best?

2 Listen to Sofia talking to her friends. What question does she ask?

....

....

3 Sofia fills in the chart like this:

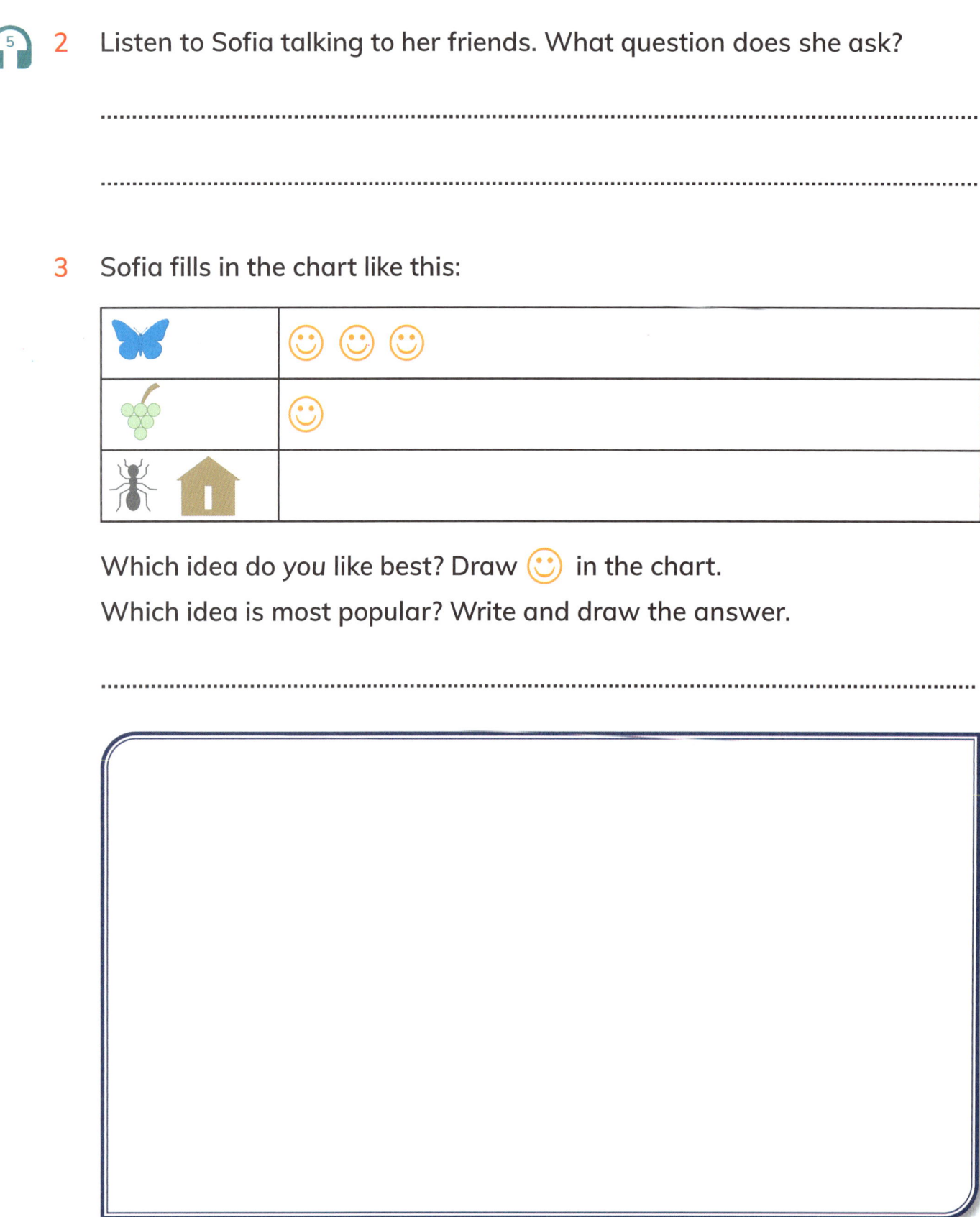

Which idea do you like best? Draw 🙂 in the chart.

Which idea is most popular? Write and draw the answer.

....

2 What kind of garden would be best?

What questions can we ask?

1 Now you are going to find out what the children in your class would like to have in a school garden.

Talk about the question you will ask. Write the words.

> Would you like .... ,
> ....
> or .... ?

2 Make a chart like the one that Sofia made.
Put pictures of your own garden ideas in the chart.

What did we find out?

1 Ask your questions to three or more children.
Put their answer in the chart. Put your own answer in the chart too.

2 Which idea is most popular? Write and draw the answer.

....

41

2 What kind of garden would be best?

> 2.3 Where can I find more facts and ideas?

Learning goals		
Our learning goals	I think	My teacher thinks
I can choose a good source of facts and ideas about gardens	☺ ☹	☺ ☹ ....

What do we need to find out?

1. Sofia and her friends want plants for butterflies in their garden. Which of these questions will help Sofia? Draw a line from the butterfly to the best question.

   Can spiders swim?

   What plants do butterflies like?

   How fast do butterflies fly?

2. Remember your most popular idea for a garden. Now you need to find out some more information.

   What questions can you ask? Talk with a partner.

   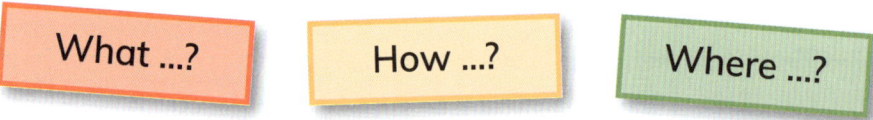

   What ...? How ...? Where ...?

2   What kind of garden would be best?

3   Write your best question on the leaf.

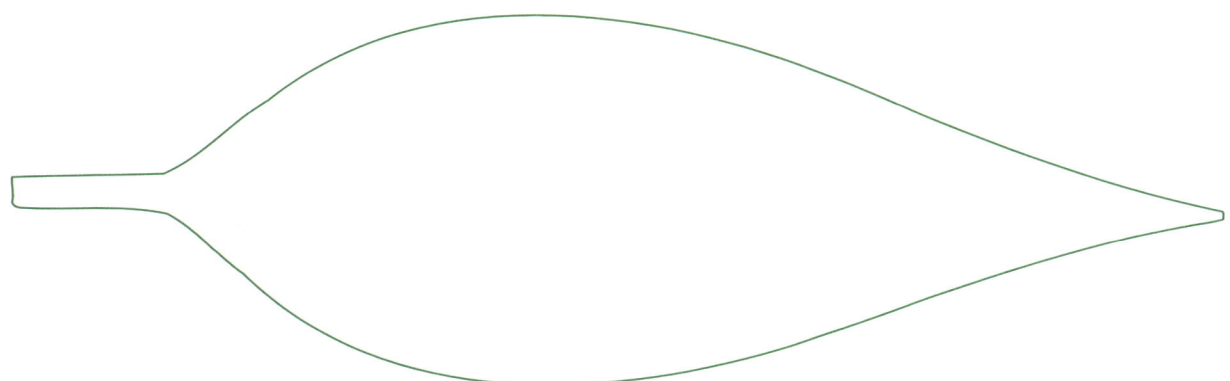

What is a good source of information?

1   If we want to find things out, we need a **source** of information.

source

Zara wants to find out how to make a school garden.
She wants lots of minibeasts to live in it. She has found some sources.

Look at each source and draw a star or a face in the box.

a very good source   ☆
quite a good source 😐
not a good source   ☹

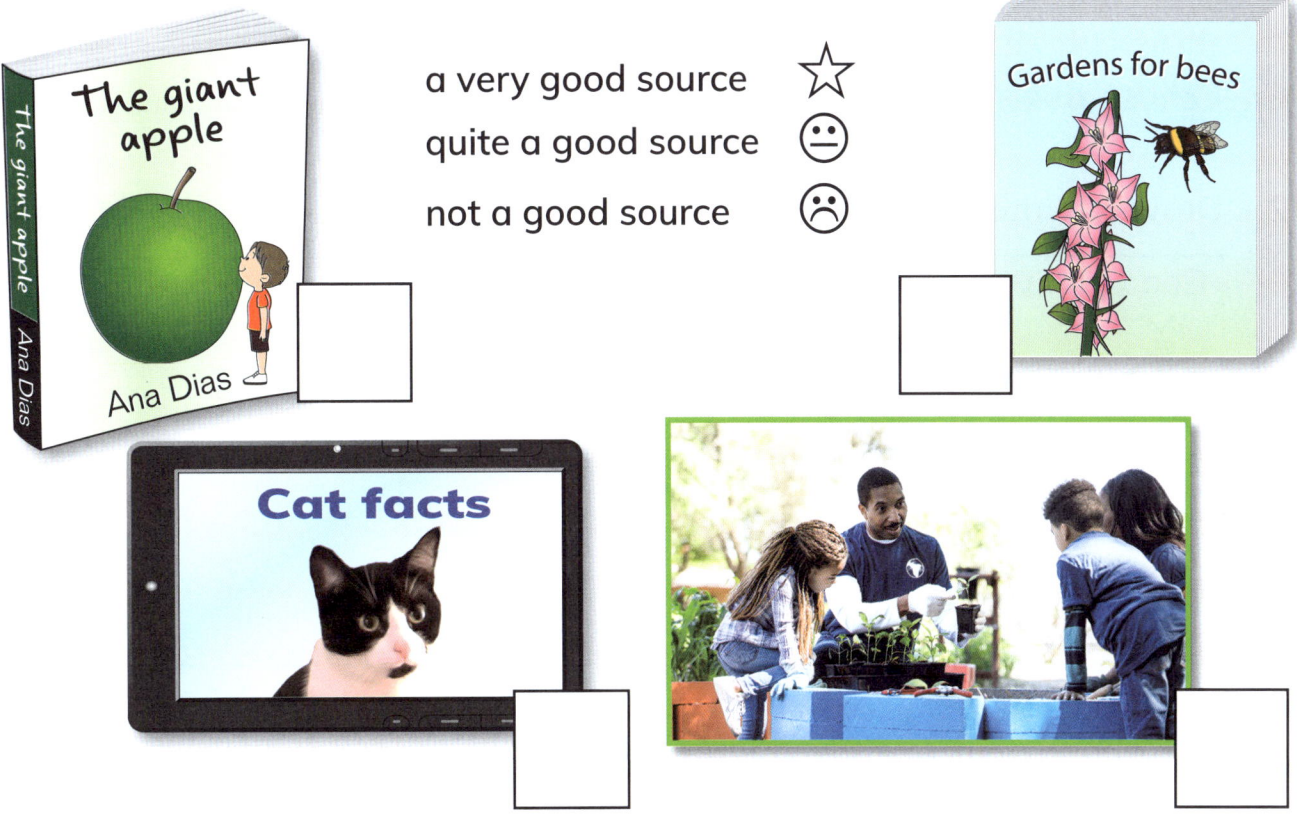

43

2 What kind of garden would be best?

2   Explain your answers to your partner. Say why.
    Here is an example:

This is not a good source because it hasn't got any ideas about gardens!

> a very good source   not a good source
> quite a good source   because

What can I find out from my own source?

1   Choose a source for yourself. Make sure it is a good source for finding facts and ideas about gardens.

    Write why you chose this source or tell your teacher.

    I chose this source because ....

2   Draw or write the things that you find out.

3   Talk about what you have found out.   **I found out ...**

2 What kind of garden would be best?

> 2.4 How can we make a model of a school garden?

Learning goals		
Our learning goals	**I think**	**My teacher thinks**
I can work with my group to make a model of a school garden	☺ 😐	☺ 😐 ....

What kind of model garden will we make?

model

1   You are going to make a **model** of a garden for your school.

   First, watch the video. You will see lots of different gardens. Think about these questions.

   a   How are the gardens different from each other?

   b   Where are the plants growing in each garden?

2   With a partner, talk about your answers to the questions.

3   (Circle) the things people can do in these gardens.

   grow something to eat   watch the birds   relax

   play football   smell the flowers

2 What kind of garden would be best?

What things will we put in our model garden?

1 Make a plan for your garden.

Tick (✓) the things people will do in your garden.

Write or draw the plants you want.

Circle the pictures of the things you want.

Our garden plan

Things to do in our garden

Grow something to eat ☐   Relax ☐

Watch the birds and other creatures ☐   Smell lovely flowers ☐

My idea: ....

Plants in our garden

....

Things in our garden

compost box

seat

bird feeder

pond

My idea:

2 What kind of garden would be best?

2. Read what Arun would like and why. Then tell your partner what you would like and why.

I would like a seat and some sunflowers. Children can sit and watch the birds eating the sunflower seeds. It will be a peaceful garden.

Did you know?

Did you know that plants need food? **Compost** is a very good food for plants. You can make it in a compost box in your garden. It's easy! Just put your banana skins, apple cores and vegetable peel in the box. Mix it up with a spade. It all gets broken down by nature, like minibeasts. After a few months, you will have lovely compost!

How should we work together?

1. Your teacher will give you some things to make your model garden with. You will work with a group. Read Zara's rule for working together well.

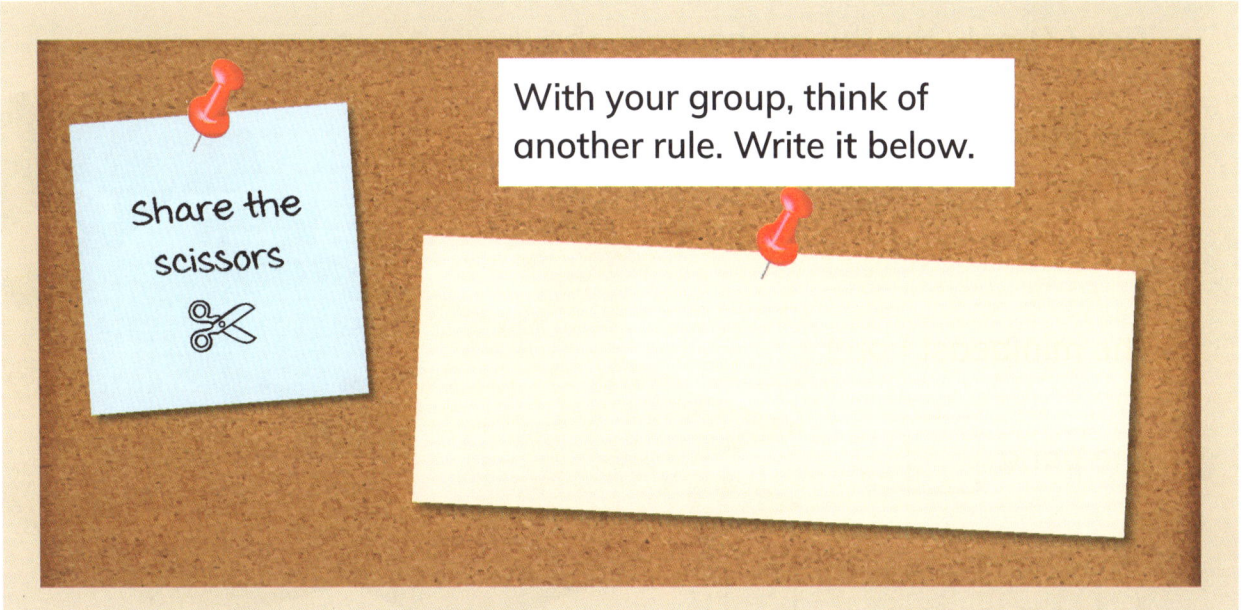

Share the scissors

With your group, think of another rule. Write it below.

2. Now make your model garden with your group.

2   What kind of garden would be best?

> 2.5 How can we tell other children about our model?

Learning goals		
Our learning goals	**I think**	**My teacher thinks**
I can talk about our model gardens	☺ 😐	☺ 😐 ....

How can we tell other children about our model garden?

1   Look at the picture of Sofia and Arun's model garden. They are telling Marcus about their model.

Listen to what they say.

Tick (✓) only the things they talk about.

favourite

The flowers ☐

The apple tree ☐

The minibeast hotel ☐

The pond ☐

Something you can do in the garden ☐

48

2 What kind of garden would be best?

2 Listen again. Answer these questions with your partner.

    a   Why did Sofia and Arun make a small garden?

    b   Why do they think their garden is good?

Talk about your answers with a partner.

3 Talk about your model garden with your group.
What will you tell other children about it?

Remember to: Say how you made your garden.

                            Say why it is a good garden.

                            Say what your favourite thing is.

What questions will we ask?

1 Look at Sofia and Arun's garden again.

Marcus wants to find out more about their garden.

He thinks of three questions.

Draw 🙂 next to the good questions.

Draw ☹ next to a question that is not useful.

How did you make the tree?

How old are you?

Do butterflies like these flowers?

2　What kind of garden would be best?

2　Think of three more good questions to ask another group about their garden.

> How did you make ...?   What is this for?
> What kind of ...?   Why ...?

Talk about your ideas with a partner. Write your questions.

....

....

....

What can we find out from other children's models?

1　Work with another group who made a different model garden. Follow the instructions.

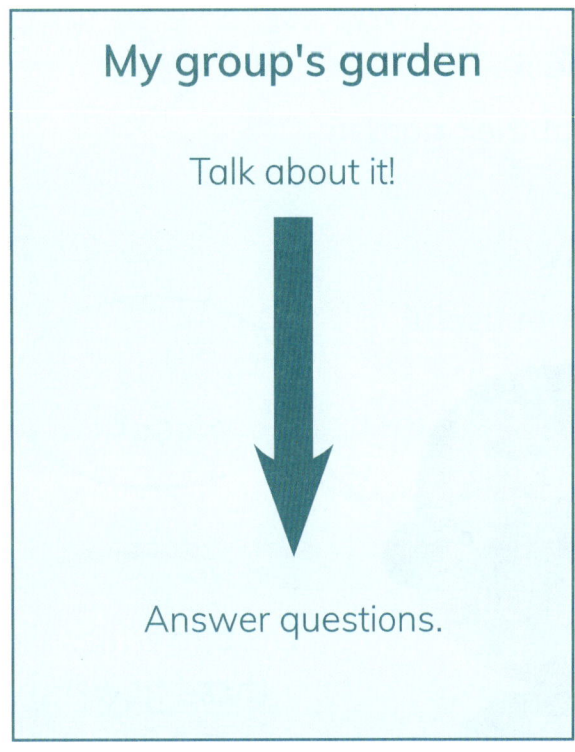

My group's garden

Talk about it!

Answer questions.

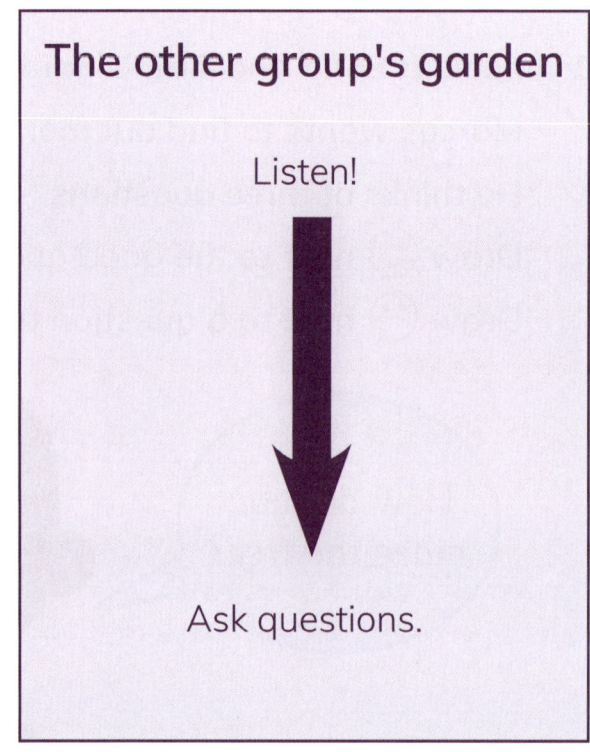

The other group's garden

Listen!

Ask questions.

2 What kind of garden would be best?

2 What is your favourite thing in the other group's garden?
Write and draw it here.

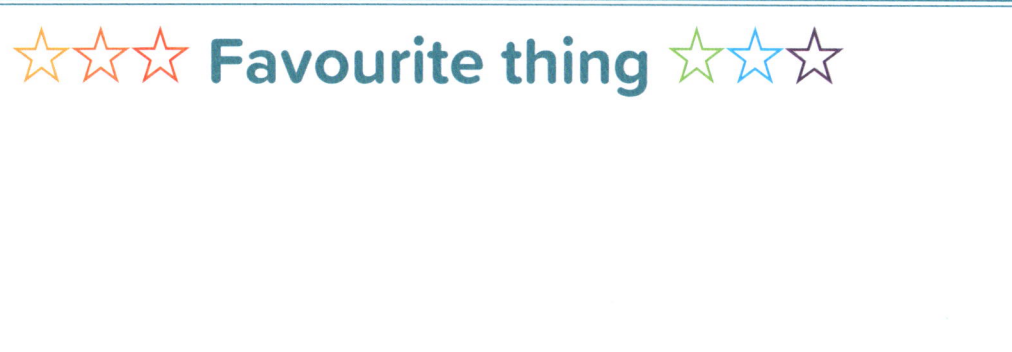

☆☆☆ **Favourite thing** ☆☆☆

My favourite thing is ...   I like it because ...

> 2.6 What have we learned?

Learning goals		
Our learning goals	**I think**	**My teacher thinks**
I can talk about what I learned	☺ 😐	☺ 😐
I can talk about something I liked	☺ 😐	☺ 😐

51

2 What kind of garden would be best?

What do I know now?

What have you found out in this project?
Write or draw two things in each box.

Things I know now about gardens	
Plants	Creatures that live in gardens
Good things to do in gardens	Good things to put in gardens

2 What kind of garden would be best?

What did I enjoy doing?

Talk about the things you did in the project.
The pictures may help you remember.
Say if you enjoyed them.

> I enjoyed …
> I quite liked …
> I didn't really enjoy …

What have I learned how to do?

Arun learned how to do something in his project.

He wrote it on a caterpillar! Read what he wrote.

I have learned how to find a good source.

Write one thing you learned how to do.

I have learned how to

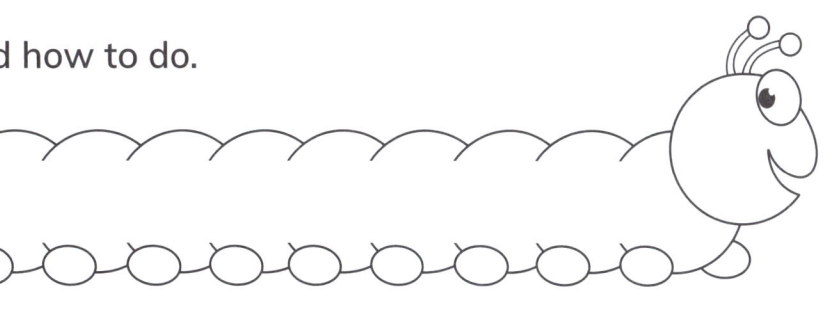

3 What do we know about jobs?

Getting started

1. Look at the picture of a building site.
   Point and say the things you can see.

   What are these people making?

2. Read and listen to the chant.

   Repeat the chant out loud.
   Act out what the workers are doing in the picture!

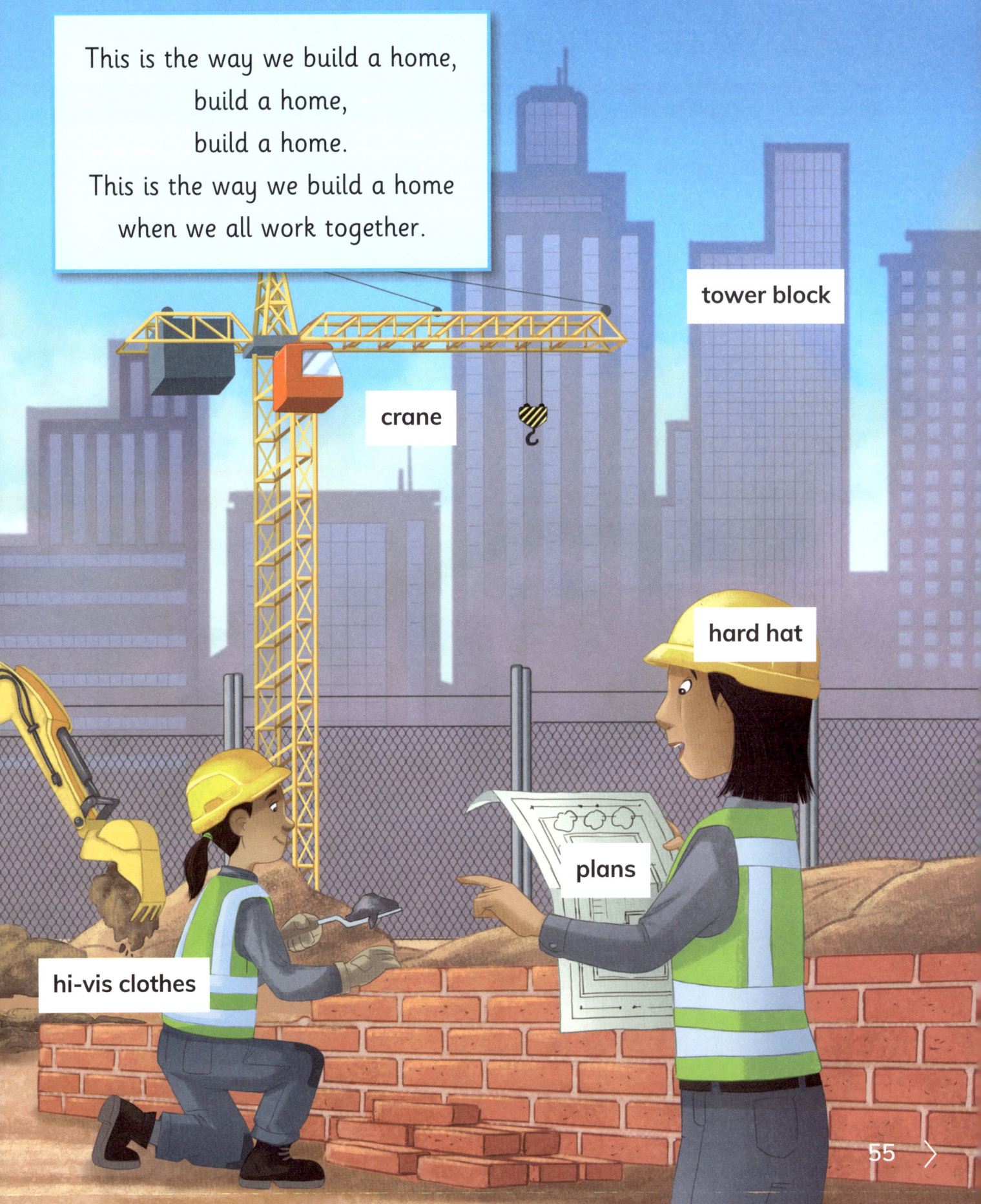

3 What do we know about jobs?

> 3.1 What work do people do?

Learning goals		
Our learning goals	I think	My teacher thinks
I can talk about different jobs that people do	☺ 😐	☺ 😐

Where do people work?

A **workplace** is a place where people work. Look at these pictures of workplaces.

workplace   job

3 What do we know about jobs?

1 Ask and answer these questions with a partner.
   a   Where are the people working?
   b   What **jobs** do you think they are doing?
   c   What special things do they use to do their job?
   d   Are they wearing any special clothes?
   e   Think of three more workplaces.

> I think
> because
> maybe

What different kinds of jobs do people do?

1   Listen to the people talking about their jobs.
    Draw a line from the person to their workplace.

Jack

Emily

Shreya

office   food factory   building site

2   Finish the sentences. Use these words to help you.

Jack helps to make ……………………………

Emily is helping to build a ……………………………

Shreya helps people to fix ……………………………

tower block

computers

chocolate

57

3 What do we know about jobs?

3   Read Sofia's question. Who would be best to answer her question?

 would be the best worker for Sofia to talk to.

4   Imagine you could ask one of the three workers to give a talk in your school.

Circle the worker you would you like to invite: Jack, Emily or Shreya?

What question would you like to ask them?

Tell your partner.

Is it easy to build a wall?

Who works near where I live?

Draw a worker who does their job near where you live.
Show the work they do.

Talk to your partner about the worker you have drawn.

- Where are they working?
- What are they doing?
- Do they use **tools** or machines?
- Do they wear special clothing?

tool

> 3.2 How can I find out about jobs?

Learning goals

Our learning goals	I think	My teacher thinks
I can ask questions about jobs	☺ 😐	☺ 😐 ....

What questions can I ask about jobs?

1. Marcus, Sofia, Zara and Arun are playing a game. The game is called 'What's my job?'

   Marcus is trying to guess the job that is on his hat.

   Arun, Sofia and Zara can only answer 'yes' or 'no' to the questions Marcus asks.

   Listen. What questions does Marcus ask?

2. With a partner, think of three more useful questions to ask.

   > Do I work ...?   Do I use ...?   Do I wear ...?   Am I ...?

3. Play the game 'What's my job?' You will play in a group of four. Your teacher will give one child a hat with the name of a job.

   The rest of the group will look at the job and answer the questions. You can only answer 'yes' or 'no'.

3 What do we know about jobs?

4 After the game, write down the job that was on your hat.

I was a ....

Write down a question that you asked.

....

How can I talk to someone about their job?

1 Arun, Marcus, Sofia and Zara are excited. A welder is coming to their school.

They have thought of some questions.

Two questions are about **facts**.
One question is about an **opinion**.

Which question is about an opinion?
Write **O** in the box next to it.

> **Did you know?**
>
> A welder joins pieces of metal together.
>
> She uses a special torch to make the metal very hot.

fact   opinion

Our questions

1 What things do you weld? ☐

2 How did you learn to be a welder? ☐

3 What is the best thing about your job? ☐

4 _____

2 With your partner, think of another question.
Add your question to the list above.

3 **What do we know about jobs?**

3   Who could you invite to your class to talk about their job?

Talk to your teacher about your ideas.

4   Then think of some questions to ask the person. Ask about facts and opinions.

Our visitor's job is ....

....

Our questions

1   _____

2   _____

3   _____

What did the visitor tell us?

1   Interview your visitor.

2   Write something that you have learned from them.

....

....

....

3 What do we know about jobs?

3.3 Where can I find out more about jobs?

Learning goals		
Our learning goals	**I think**	**My teacher thinks**
I can choose a good source of facts and ideas about jobs	☺ 😐	☺ 😐 ....
I can give my opinion about what I have found out	☺ 😐	☺ 😐 ....

62

3 What do we know about jobs?

What is the best source of information?

1. Zara, Arun, Marcus and Sofia have chosen jobs that they want to find out about.

Write the number of the best source for each person. The first one has been done for you.

Arun wants to find out more about: **welders** ☐ 1

Zara wants to find out about: **car workers** ☐

Marcus wants to find out about: **bakers** ☐

Sofia wants to find out about: **builders** ☐

Talk about your answers with a partner.

2. Now it's your turn to choose a job to find out about.

Later, you will do a role play about this job with your group, so you will need lots of information from good sources.
Think about a job that you have good sources for, like books or videos.

Write the job here: ....

3 What do we know about jobs?

What do we need to find out?

1 Marcus wants to find out about the job of a baker. Look at Marcus's question:

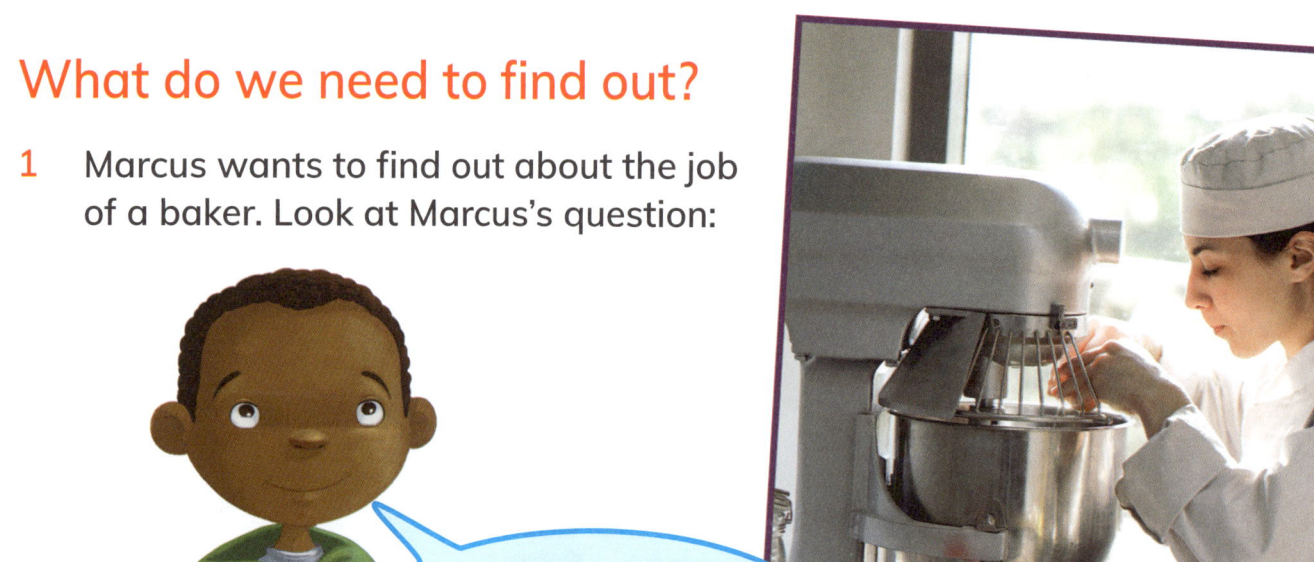

Why does a baker wear white clothes at work?

2 Now think about the job that **you** have decided to find out about with your group.

What questions can you ask about the job? Talk with your group.

3 Write your two favourite questions about the job you chose.

1 ....

....

2 ....

....

3 What do we know about jobs?

What can I find out from my own source?

1. Choose a source with good information about the job you have picked. Look at your source. What can you find out about the job you chose?

   Draw or write the things that you find out.

   Name of the job I'm finding out about: ....

What they do	People they work with
The place where they work	Things that they use

2. Talk to your group about the most interesting things that you have found out.

   In my opinion, the most interesting thing I found out was …

3 What do we know about jobs?

> 3.4 How can we do a role play about work?

Learning goals		
Our learning goals	I think	My teacher thinks
I can do a role play about work with my group	☺ 😐	☺ 😐 ....

What different jobs do people do in a workplace?

1. You are going to do a **role play** to show different jobs that people do in one workplace.

    You will work with a group.

    First, watch the video. It will give you some ideas.

    There are lots of people doing different jobs. They are all working together to make the same thing.

    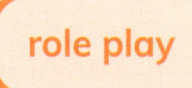

    Think about these questions.
    a   Where are the people working?
    b   Are they all doing the same job or different jobs?
    c   What are they wearing?
    d   What tools are they using?

    Talk about the questions with a partner.

66

3 What do we know about jobs?

2   Watch the video again.

Circle the things that you saw in the video. One has been circled already.

a   Taking the beans from the pods

b   Pouring the chocolate into a mould

c   Decorating the chocolate

d   Putting the chocolate in boxes

e   Eating the chocolate

Did you know?

You can use moulds to make things in different shapes. You can put water in a mould and freeze it. The ice will be the shape of the mould! You can put melted chocolate in a mould too.

Have you ever put something in a mould?

What things will we do in our role play?

1   Arun and his group are going to do a role play about workers who make cars. Their workplace will be a car factory. Read what Arun says.

Our workplace will be a car factory. We will pretend to make cars.

Write down where your group's workplace will be:

....

3   What do we know about jobs?

2   What jobs will you do in your workplace? Make a list.

3   What clothes would be good for your role play?

Draw them on the body shape.

Talk to your partner.
Tell your partner why
you need these things.

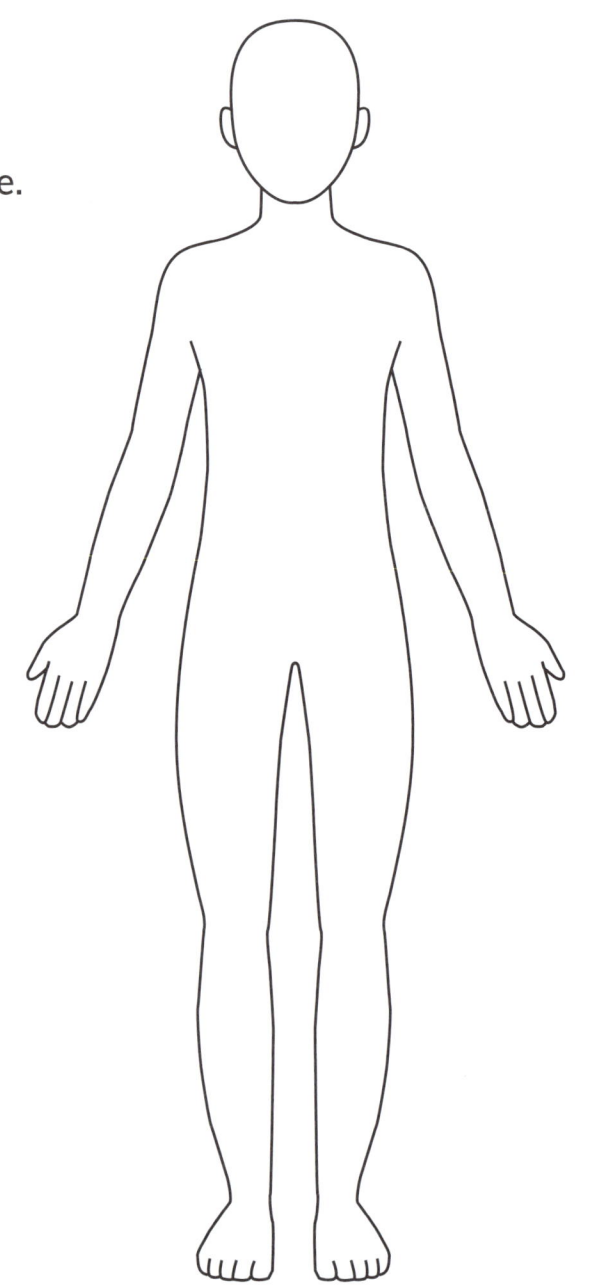

3 What do we know about jobs?

4 What other things will you need for your role play?

Put a (circle) around the tools you would like.

Or draw your own ideas.

My ideas

69

3 What do we know about jobs?

How can we work together?

1   Now you need to decide who will do what job in your role play.

Look at Arun, Sofia, Marcus and Zara's plan.

Job	Name	Picture
Fix the wheels on the car.	Arun	
Use the robot arm.	Zara	

Make a plan for your group.

First, make a list of jobs. Then write the name of the person who will do each job.

Job	Name

3   What do we know about jobs?

2   Draw a picture of you doing your job in your group's role play.

› 3.5 How can we tell other children about our workplace?

Learning goals		
Our learning goals	I think	My teacher thinks
I can talk about our workplace	☺ 😐	☺ 😐

3 What do we know about jobs?

What shall we say in our role play?

1. Look at the picture of Zara, Sofia, Arun and Marcus doing their role play. They are telling other children about their ideas for the factory and the jobs they are doing.

   Listen to what they say.

   Tick (✓) only the things they talk about.

   Putting on the wheels ☐   Operating the robot arm ☐

   Putting in the pedals ☐   Buying more parts ☐

   Putting in the seats ☐

3 What do we know about jobs?

2 Look at the picture and listen again.
Answer these questions with your partner.

a What is Arun's job?

b What did the children find out about robots?

c What is Marcus doing?

Talk about your answers with a partner.

3 Now think about your group's role play.

What will you tell another group of children about the jobs you are doing?

Talk with your group.
What will each person say?

Ideas

Say what jobs you are doing.

Say what tools or machines you are using.

Say why it is like a real workplace.

In our role play, I will say ....

What questions will we ask?

1 Zara, Arun, Marcus and Sofia have done their role play. Their friends want to find out more about the work that they do in the car factory. They have thought of three questions.

Draw  next to the good questions.

Draw  next to a question that is not useful.

What colour is the factory?

What machines do you use in your factory?

What other jobs are there in the factory?

> 3 What do we know about jobs?

2 Think of three more good questions to ask Zara, Sofia, Marcus and Arun about their workplace.

> What is ... for?
> What is your favourite ...?
> Why do you have to wear ...?
> Why ...?
> How do you use a ...?

Talk about your ideas with a partner. Write your questions.

....

....

....

What can we find out from other children's role plays?

1 Work with another group who made a different workplace. Follow the instructions.

My group's role play

Do your role play!

↓

Answer questions.

Another group's role play

Watch their role play!

↓

Ask questions.

74

3 What do we know about jobs?

2 What was the most interesting thing that you learned about jobs?
Give your opinion.
Write and draw it below:

The most interesting thing I learned about jobs

....

....

3 What do we know about jobs?

> 3.6 What have we learned about jobs?

Learning goals

Our learning goals	I think	My teacher thinks
I can talk about what I learned	☺ 😐	☺ 😐
I can say what I did to help my group	☺ 😐	☺ 😐

What do I know now?

What have you found out in this project?
Write or draw two things in each box.

Things I know now about jobs	
Jobs people do 	Places where people work 
Tools and machines that workers use 	Special clothes that workers wear 

3   What do we know about jobs?

How did I help my group?

1   Talk about the things you did together in the project. The pictures may help you remember.

2   Zara helped her group. Read what she says.

I helped to make a robot arm. I put a glove on the arm. The glove was my idea.

I worked with .....

I helped my group to ...

Say what you did to help your group.

3 What do we know about jobs?

What have I learned how to do?

Sofia learned how to do something in her project. She wrote it on a spanner!

I have learned how to tell people what car workers do.

Write one thing you learned how to do.

I have learned how to

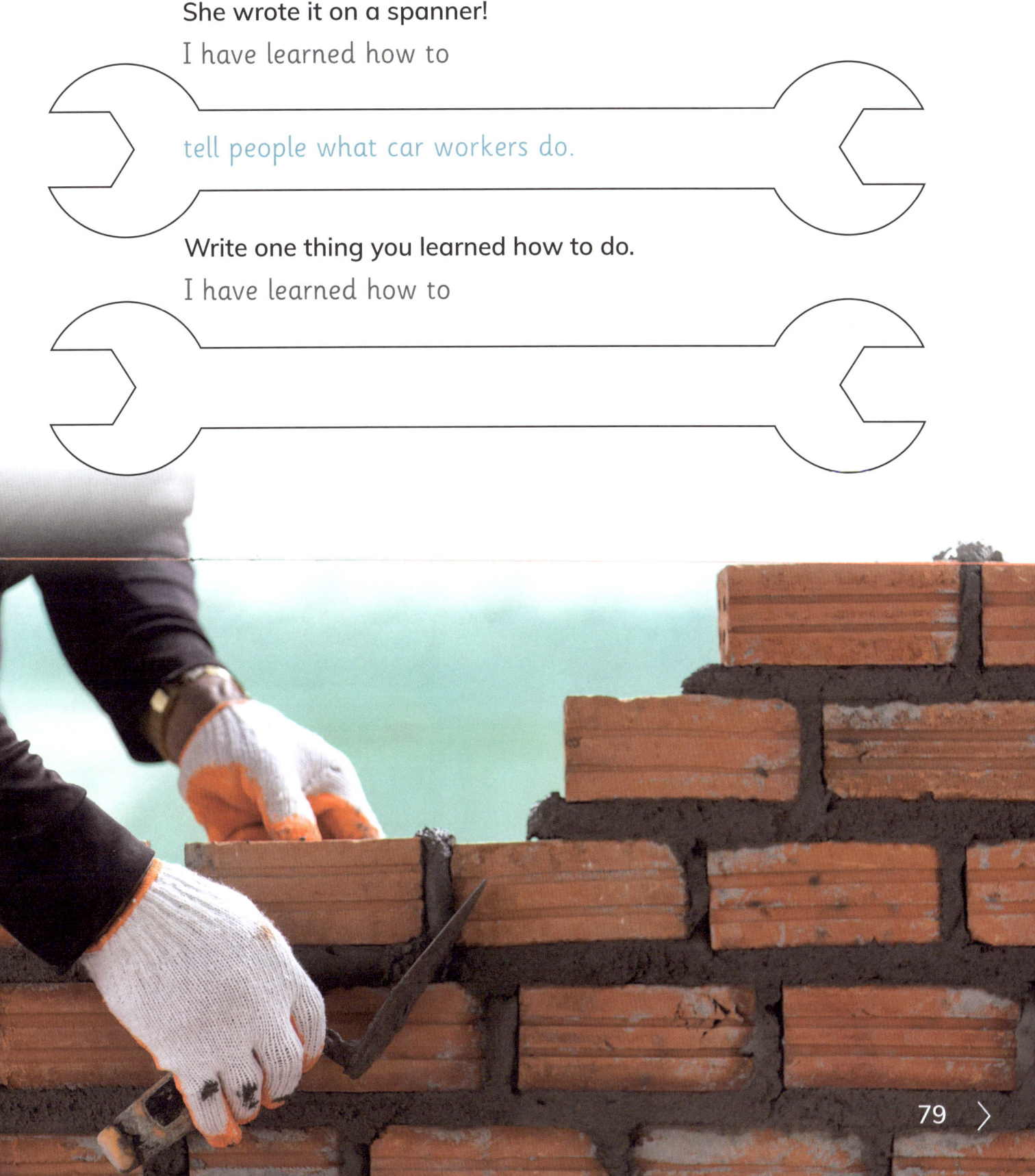

4 How can we save water?

Getting started

1. Look at this picture.
   What do you think the children are doing?
   Talk to a partner.
2. What do we need water for? The picture will give you some ideas.

4   How can we save water?

We need water so that we can …

81

4 How can we save water?

4.1 How do we use water at school?

Learning goals

Our learning goals	I think	My teacher thinks
I can talk about where we use water at school	☺ 😐	☺ 😐
I can talk about what happens when I do things	☺ 😐	☺ 😐

Where do we use water in school?

We use water in school for lots of reasons. Water comes out of taps.

Marcus and Zara have been counting the taps in their school. They have marked them on a map.

Some taps were dripping.
Why is a dripping tap not good?

4 How can we save water?

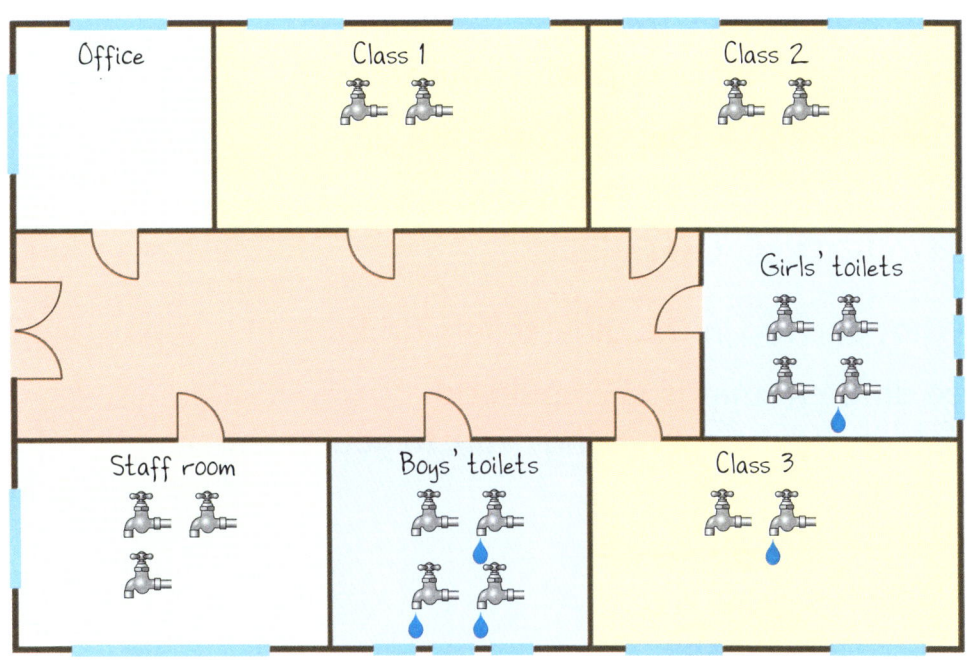

1   Look at Marcus and Zara's map. Answer the questions.

   a   Which rooms have four taps?

   ....

   ....

   b   Which rooms have two taps?

   ....

   ....

   c   Which room has no taps?

   ....

   d   Which rooms have taps that drip?

   ....

   ....

83

4 How can we save water?

2   Which rooms in your school have taps?
Write a list or draw the taps on a map with your teacher.

Which taps drip? Draw a drip under the taps that drip.

What is the best thing to do?

1   Zara has noticed that one tap in the girls' toilets drips.

She thinks of three different things she could do.
What would happen if she did each thing? Talk to your partner.

1 She could put the plug in.

2 She could leave the plug out.

3 She could tell a member of staff.

Excuse me. The tap in the girls' toilets is dripping.

2   What would you do if you found a dripping tap?

I would ....

4   How can we save water?

Why do we use water in school?

1   Sofia and Arun have been thinking about why they use water in school.

They answered some questions. Read what they wrote.

How did you use water?	I watered the plant.
Why?	The leaves were yellow. The soil was dry.
What happened?	After a week the plant was green and healthy.

How did you use water?	I filled my water bottle. I had a drink.
Why?	It was hot. I ran a lot. I got very thirsty.
What happened?	I was not thirsty any more.

4 How can we save water?

2   Answer the same questions as Sofia and Arun.

How did you use water? ....

....

Why? ....

....

What happened? ....

....

> 4.2 How do other people use water?

Learning goals

Our learning goals	I think	My teacher thinks
I can find out about how people use water	☺ 😐	☺ 😐
I can record information in a chart	☺ 😐	☺ 😐

4 How can we save water?

How can we talk to people about using water?

1   Arun, Sofia, Zara and Marcus have been talking to three different people. They asked them how they use water. Look at the photos. Can you guess how each person uses water? Talk to your partner.

The school cook

Arun's friend

Sofia's neighbour

87

4 How can we save water?

 2 Now listen to the people talking about how they use water.
Did you guess right? Write the answers.

a The school cook uses water to ....

   and to ....

b Arun's friend uses water to ....

   ....

c Sofia's neighbour uses water to ....

   ....

How can we find out more?

Arun, Sofia, Zara and Marcus wanted to know more.
They wanted to collect some facts about how much water people use.

1 Sofia's neighbour waters the plants in his garden.
   She talked to him about this.

   She made a chart to show what he told her.

   What can we find out from Sofia's chart? Tell your partner.

Morning	Midday	Evening	Night
🪣		🪣	

Write when Sofia's neighbour waters his plants.

Sofia's neighbour waters his plants

....

and ....

88

4 How can we save water?

2   Arun's friend fills her rabbit's water bottle.

What question could Arun ask his friend?

Arun talked to his friend. He made a chart to show what his friend said.

What can we find out from Arun's chart? He put a water bottle in the chart every time his friend filled the water bottle. Tell your partner.

Monday	Tuesday	Wednesday	Thursday
🍼	🍼🍼	🍼	🍼🍼

Friday	Saturday	Sunday
🍼	🍼🍼	🍼🍼🍼

How many times did Arun's friend fill up her rabbit's water bottle last week?

....

4 How can we save water?

How can we show people what we found out?

1 Think about how your family uses water.
   Tick (✓) the things that people in your family do.

   Have a shower ☐

   Have a bath ☐

   Brush their teeth ☐

   Wash clothes ☐

   Something else: ☐

   ....

2 Choose one of the things in the list. Put a ⬭circle⬯ around it.

   You are going to talk about it to somebody in your family.
   You will find out how often they do the thing you chose.

   I will talk to ....

   What question will you ask?

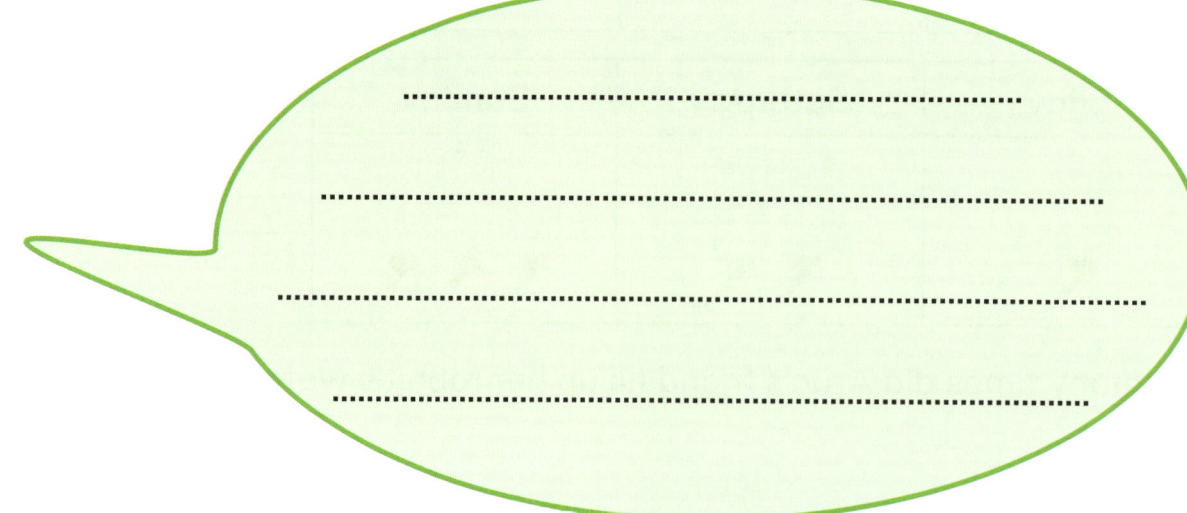

90

4   How can we save water?

3   You are going to put your facts in a chart.
    Look again at Sofia's chart and Arun's chart.

    a   Which chart will be better for your facts?

        Write 1 or 2: ....

    b   What picture will you draw in the chart? Draw it here.

Chart 1

Morning	Midday	Evening	Night

Chart 2

Monday	Tuesday	Wednesday	Thursday

Friday	Saturday	Sunday

4   Make a chart. Collect your facts.
    Draw your picture into your chart to show your facts.

4 How can we save water?

> 4.3 What do I think about saving water?

Learning goals

Our learning goals	I think	My teacher thinks
I can say what I think about saving water	☺ 😐	☺ 😐

What can we find out about saving water?

1   Arun does not know about saving water.
    Read what he says.

My friend says there is too much water in some places. He says we don't need to save water.

Is Arun's friend right? What would you say to Arun?

 2   Watch the video about water.

Circle **Yes**, **No** or **I'm not sure** for the sentences below.

a   There is a lot of water on the Earth.   Yes   No   I'm not sure

b   We can drink the water in the sea.   Yes   No   I'm not sure

c   It is very important to look after our water.   Yes   No   I'm not sure

4 How can we save water?

3   Watch the video again. Then answer the questions with your partner.

  a   What happens if there isn't enough clean water?

  b   How can we **save** water?

> **Did you know?**
>
> Clouds are made of water. When clouds cool down, it starts to rain.

Why should we save water?

1   Marcus has been making some notes about why we should save water. His ideas have got mixed up. Can you help him join his ideas back up? The first one has been done for you.

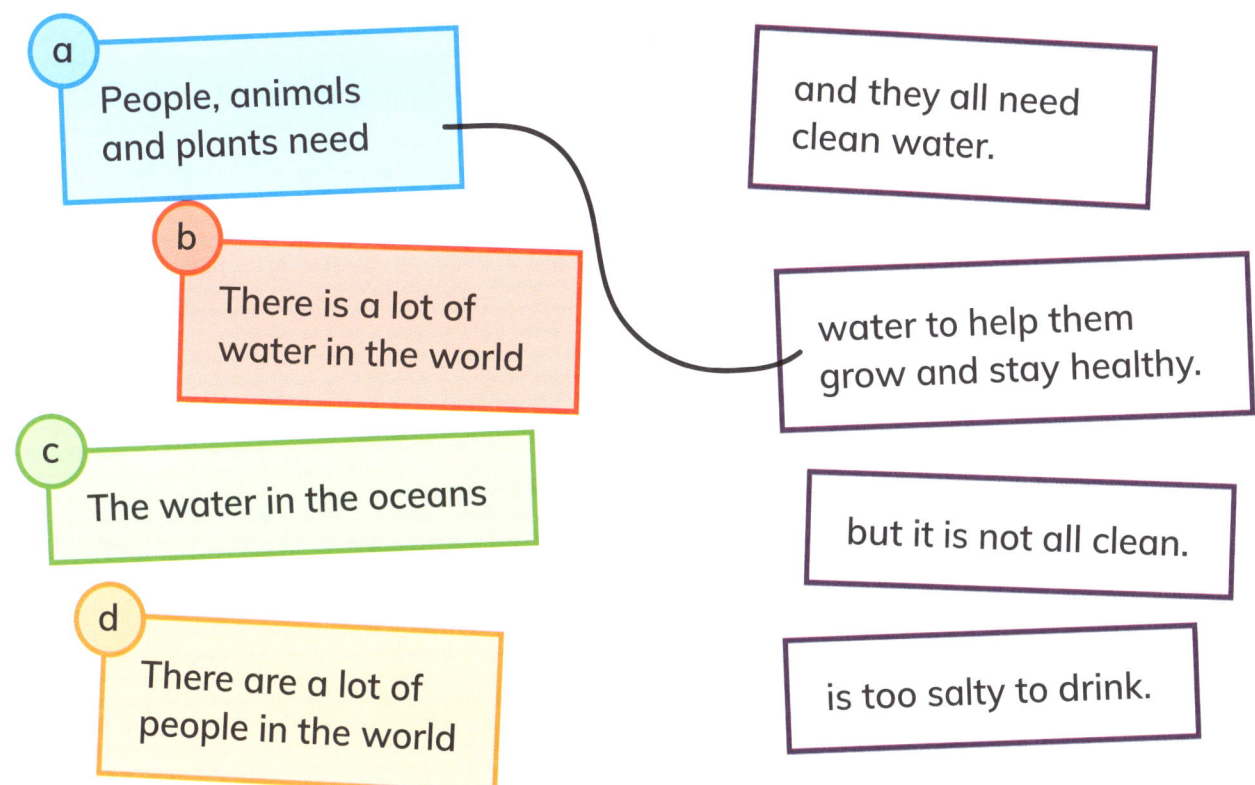

a   People, animals and plants need — water to help them grow and stay healthy.

b   There is a lot of water in the world — but it is not all clean.

c   The water in the oceans — is too salty to drink.

d   There are a lot of people in the world — and they all need clean water.

4 How can we save water?

How can I say what I think about saving water?

Marcus and Zara have now seen a video about saving water.
They have thought about why they should save water.
They have given their opinion.

Saving water is important to me because I love paddling in the pool.

Saving water is important to me because sometimes there is not enough to water our plants.

1   Can you think of a reason why saving water is important to you?
    Write your opinion below:

    I think we should save water because ....

    ....

    ....

    Compare your answers with your partner.
    Are your opinions the same or different?

4.4 What different ways are there to save water?

Learning goals		
Our learning goals	**I think**	**My teacher thinks**
I can work with my group to ask and answer questions about saving water	☺ 😐	☺ 😐

How can we save water?

1   Look at the two photos. Answer the questions.

   a   What are the people washing?

   They are washing ....

   b   In which photo is the person saving water?

   Draw a star ☆ in the box next to this photo.

4 How can we save water?

2   Look at the two photos. Answer the questions.

a   What are the people washing?

They are washing ....

b   In which photo is the person saving water?

Draw a star ☆ in the box next to this photo.

Did you know?

You can turn the tap off when you brush your teeth. This can save enough water to fill about ten water bottles like this one.

How can pictures show people how to save water?

1. Look at the pictures. They tell us more ways to save water.
   What do you think each picture tells us to do?
   Write it next to the picture.

1 ....
....
....

2 ....
....
....

3 ....
....
....

2. Think of another way to save water or **reuse** water. What picture could you draw to tell people how to use water carefully? Draw your picture.

reuse

4 How can we save water?

How can we talk about saving water in our group?

1. Work with a group. You will need the picture that you drew.
   Follow the instructions. Take turns to speak and listen.

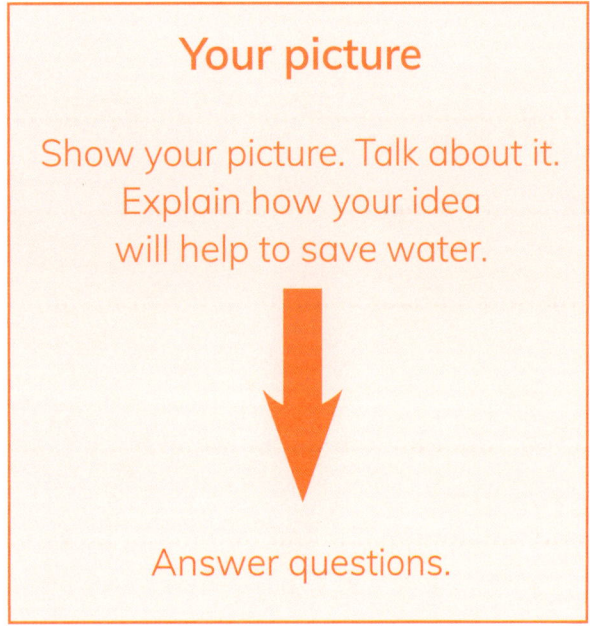

2. Look at all your group's pictures together.
   Which is the best idea for saving water?

   The best idea for saving water is ....

   ....

   Why do you think it is a good idea?

   It is a good idea because ....

   ....

   ....

4 How can we save water?

> 4.5 How can we tell other people how to use water carefully?

Learning goals

Our learning goals	I think	My teacher thinks
I can tell other people about using water carefully	☺ 😐	☺ 😐 ....

How could we do a show and tell?

4 How can we save water?

You are going to do a **show and tell** for an **audience**. An audience is a group of people who watch and listen.

> **show and tell**
> **audience**

First, let's get some ideas from Arun, Sofia, Marcus and Zara. They did a show and tell. Their audience was a group of children from another class. Some parents came too. Their show and tell was about saving water.

1. Look at the picture. Talk to a partner.

   a What are the children holding?

   b Why do you think they are holding these things?

   c What do you think they are going to tell their audience?

2. Arun, Sofia, Marcus and Zara wanted to tell their audience their idea for saving water. Listen to what they said.

   What do Arun, Sofia, Marcus and Zara want their audience to do? Tick (✓) the right answer.

   Wash their vegetables in a watering can. ☐

   Use the same water for washing vegetables and watering plants. ☐

3. If you could ask the group a question about their idea, what would you ask them?

   Write your question here.

   ....

   ....

   ....

   ....

4 How can we save water?

4 They finished their show and tell with something for their audience to remember. Listen and join in!

waste

We save water.	We try not to **waste** it.
We save water.	We try not to waste it.
So can you!	You can, too!
So can you!	You can, too!

What shall we do in our show and tell?

1 Now think about your own show and tell.

Who will your audience be?

....

2 Talk to your group. What do you want your audience to do? How do you want them to save water?

Think of some ideas about what you can show. Draw your ideas here.

101

4 How can we save water?

3 Think about what your group will say.
In your notebook, write the name of each person in your group. Write what they will say.

> We need water to ...
> You can save water if you ...
> Some people waste water when ...

What will our audience see and hear?

1 You want your audience to understand what you say to them. How can you make sure that they see and hear you clearly?

Read the list of tips. Add one more tip to the list.

Tips for speaking to an audience

Look at the audience when you speak.

Say your words clearly.

Make your voice sound interesting.

....

....

4　How can we save water?

2　Practise reading this sentence to your partner. Say it clearly, in an interesting voice. Look at your partner when you are speaking. Then your partner will read the sentence to you.

> It is easy to save water.

Answer the questions about your partner. Tick (✓) the things they did.

Did your partner speak clearly? ☐

Did your partner speak in an interesting voice? ☐

Did your partner look at you while speaking? ☐

If they did not, try again!

3　Now think about the actions you will do in your show and tell. Practise them with your group.

Are your actions clear? Will your audience understand what you are showing?

4 How can we save water?

› 4.6 What have we learned about sharing ideas?

Learning goals		
Our learning goals	I think	My teacher thinks
I can talk about what I learned	☺ 😐	☺ 😐 ....
I can talk about how somebody helped me	☺ 😐	☺ 😐 ....

104 ›

4 How can we save water?

What do I know now?

What have you found out in this project?
Write or draw two things in each box.

Things I know now about water	
How we use water	**How people waste water**
Things we can do to save and reuse water	**How to tell our ideas to an audience**

4 How can we save water?

What have we done together?

1. With a partner, talk about the things you have done with other children in this project.

    The pictures may help you remember.

    - Say if you enjoyed working with other children to do these things.
    - Say what was hard.
    - Say if you are proud of something you did with other children.

2. Write your answers.

    I enjoyed doing ....

    with ....

    I found it hard to ....

    I am proud that we ....

4 How can we save water?

Who helped me?

Zara thought about her saving water project.
She thought about someone who helped her.
She wrote her idea on a washing-up bowl!

..Marcus........... helped me to   draw the taps on our map

Write one thing that somebody in your group helped you to do.

.... helped me to   ....

How have we been good learners?

Sofia, Marcus, Arun and Zara have been thinking about how they have been good learners in this project.

This is what Zara wrote:

I was brave. I said my own words in the show and tell.

When were you brave in your project?

....

This is what Arun wrote:

I had an idea. I showed people where the water runs away.

When did you have an idea for your project?

....

Glossary

audience	people watching a show or event
chart	a way of showing information clearly
different	not the same
display	writing and pictures for people to look at
fact	something that you know is true
family member	a person who is part of your family
favourite	a thing that someone likes the most
festival	a special day for celebration
grateful	when you want to say thank you to someone
interview	a conversation where one person asks questions and the other person gives answers
job	the work that someone does that they get paid to do
minibeast hotel	a garden object built to be a home for small creatures (such as bees, butterflies and snails)
model	a small object that is made so that it looks like a bigger thing, like a model boat
opinion	you give an opinion when you say what you think about something
popular	if something is popular, it means that lots of people like it
reuse	use something again
role play	when you role play, you pretend to be another person
same	exactly like
save	stop something being thrown away or wasted
show and tell	an activity where a child brings something into school and talks about it

similar	quite like something else in some way
source	something that has facts or information about a topic, like a book or a website
taught	shown how to do something, or told something
tool	a thing that people need to do their job, like a hammer
waste	to use too much of something or use something badly
workplace	a place where people do jobs, like factories, offices or shops

Acknowledgements

The authors and publishers acknowledge the following sources of copyright material and are grateful for the permissions granted. While every effort has been made, it has not always been possible to identify the sources of all the material used, or to trace all copyright holders. If any omissions are brought to our notice, we will be happy to include the appropriate acknowledgements on reprinting.

Thanks to the following for permission to reproduce images:

Cover image: Pablo Gallego/Beehive Illustration

P1 Thomas Barwick/GI(x2); RealisticFilm/GI; ImagesBazaar/GI; FG Trade/GI; FPG/GI; Keystone/GI; Beeldbewerking/GI; Jose Luis Pelaez Inc/GI; **P2** Caia Image/GI; Uniquely india/GI; Halfpoint Images/GI; Luis Alvarez/GI; Renate Wefers/GI; FG Trade/GI; Martin Wahlborg/GI; Per Magnus Persson/GI; Dougal Waters/GI; Tomekbudujedomek/GI; K-Kwanchai/GI; SDI Productions/GI; kali9/GI; Francesco Vaninetti Photo/GI; Goglik83/GI; GaryAlvis/GI; Savoilic/GI; **P3** Tdub303/GI; Alvarez/GI; Monty Rakusen/GI(x2); InStock/GI; AleksandarGeorgiev/GI; Deepak Sethi/GI; Hero Images/GI; Xavierarnau/GI; Mgstudyo/GI; iz ustun/GI; Education Images/GI(x2); cako74/GI; Nick David/GI; AJ_Watt/GI; Zzvet/GI; AYImages/GI; Morsa Images/GI; AlexSava/GI; Weiquan Lin/GI; Antagain/GI; PeopleImages/GI; Pramote Polyamate/GI; **P4** Ansonsaw/GI; XiXinXing/GI; Ozgurcankaya/GI; Lawrence Manning/GI; Jxfzsy/GI; Hadynyah/GI; PhotoAlto/Anne-Sophie Bost/GI; Cavan Images/GI; John D. Buffington/GI; Stefania Pelfini, La Waziya Photography/GI; Dmytro Lukyanets/GI; S-cphoto/GI; Yasser Chalid/GI.

Key: GI = Getty Images.